NLP

Techniques Of Neuro Linguistic Programming For Communicating With Your Inner Self And Taking Charge Of Your Future

(The Most Reliable Resource For Mastering Covert Techniques Of Mind Control And The Finer Points Of The Persuasive Arts)

JanuszEdlinger

TABLE OF CONTENT

The Idea Of The Unlightened Side Of Human Consciousness 1

What Is NLP And How Does It Work? 10

What Is Hypnotic Language Patterns Such An Essential Topic? 18

Here Are Some Illustrations Of Hypnotic Language Patterns That You Can Start Using Today! 27

Developing Anchors That Are Both Powerful And Beneficial 31

Ignoring Unfavorable Events And Experiences 38

The Skill Of Influencing One's Own Behavior Via The Use Of Neurolinguistic Processing, Often Known As Nlp 45

The 5 Keys To NLP Success 49

You Can Get What You Want If You Ask Enough Questions 55

How To Apply NLP In Your Everyday Life 66

NLP Benefits 75

The Various Forms Of NLP Instruction 81

- NLP Is An Abbreviation For Neuro-Linguistic Programming. 87
- Principal Forms And Methods Of Manipulation 92
- Sinister Influence And The Art Of Manipulation 103
- Training And Certificates In NLP Are Available Here 108
- Persuasion 112
- Persuasion 123
- The Numerous Advantages Of NLP Training 136
- Strategy For Acquiring Knowledge 140
- NLP And Several Other Forms Of Coaching .. 145

The Idea Of The Unlightened Side Of Human Consciousness

Dark psychology is the study of the human experience, and it refers to the psychological goal of those who prey on the psychological well-being of others. The human race is capable of victimizing other humans as well as other living creatures. Despite the fact that some people repress or ignore their urges, others give in to them and act accordingly. The field of study known as "Dark Psychology" makes an effort to understand the ideas, emotions, and beliefs that lead to the conduct of human predators.

Dark Psychology is based on the idea that growth almost always, if not always, serves a rational, goal-oriented purpose and that it is always deliberate. The remaining 0.01% of Dark Psychology is concerned with the violent victimization of another individual who cannot be purposefully targeted, well defined by biological theory, or morally justified by ideology. Therefore, if you want to avoid the shadowy side of the human mind, you should be wary of yourself and anybody else around you who has such tendencies.

iPredator If they are not stopped, ipredators and other acts of thievery, cruelty, and harassment will become a global trend and a societal concern in the next age. The many departments of iPredator include those that deal with cyber sexual predators, cyber-bullies, cyber-threats, cyber-stalkers, cyber-criminals, and cyber warfare engaged in by religious or political extremists. The concept of iPredator is similar to that of Dark Psychology in that it places all forms of deviant and criminal behavior on a scale based on the degree of the offense and the intent behind it; however, iPredator expands this framework to include violence, harassment, and cyber victimization that occurs via the use of ICT. The following is what is included in the iPredator description:

A person, community, or nation that uses information and communication technologies (ICTs) to participate in activities such as abuse, victimization, intimidation, harassment, robbery, or dismissal of others, either directly or indirectly. Deviant impulses, cravings for perceptual distortions, domination, power, religious fanaticism, vengeance, political repression, mental disease, social recognition, or psychological and financial advantage are what fuel the iPredators. iPredators may be of any age or ethnicity, and they are not deterred by factors such as socioeconomic standing, spiritual or national identity, or ethnicity or nationality. iPredator is, in fact, a worldwide term that is used to identify individuals who make use of information and communication technologies (ICT) in order to engage in aggressive, manipulative, deviant, or destructive actions. The core tenet of this concept is that psychopathological categories that are alien to mankind include people who commit crimes via the internet, people who are psychotic, and those who are severely disturbed.

An incendiary

That particular person has an unhealthy preoccupation with kindling and maintaining fires. These individuals also had a childhood filled with sexual and physical abuse at various points in their development. The trait of being alone, having few acquaintances, and being fully fascinated with the act of setting fires and causing destruction is characteristic of a significant number of serial arsonists. Arsonists who ignite several fires tend to become highly ritualistic and to continue displaying stereotyped views on the ways in which they start fires. Arsonists typically boast and concentrate on the design of their fire starting episodes because they are concerned about the fire setting. A significant number of people who set fires feel sexually aroused up to the point when they set their target on fire, at which point they continue to masturbate while watching the burn. Given the compulsive and ritualistic nature of the arsonist's methods, the prolific arsonist derives joy from his deeds.

To engage in necrophilia

Necrologies, thanatophobia, and necrophilia are all terms that refer to the same sort of disturbed person. There are males in the world who become sexually aroused by dead bodies, and they really exist. Paraphilia is another word that may be used to refer to necrophilia. The medical term "paraphilia" is used to describe a person's sexual arousal and concern with items, circumstances, or individuals that are not components of subjective stimuli but which may elicit major difficulties or discomfort in such a person. This term was derived from the term "paraphilia," which means "paraphilic." Necrophiles experience paraphilia when they are sexually aroused by a dead person or object. This may take the form of sexual arousal. Researchers who have studied necrophiles and gathered their profiles have discovered that necrophiles have a very difficult time engaging in sexual activity with other people. In contrast to sexual connection with a real living, some people find the idea of engaging in sexual activity with a dead person to be more comforting and reassuring. Necrophiles, who are members of an organization for the dead, have shared their fantastic experiences with the rule in many conversations. When compared to the illusion of control that is essentially required, a sense of belonging does become secondary.

Criminal with a Killing Pattern

The term "serial killer" refers to a genuine human being who commits many murders during a period of thirty days or more. This individual is considered to be a real human murderer. After each death, the serial murderers go through a period of "cooling off," according to interviews with many of them. The cooling-off phase of a serial killer is a mental refractory period in which the murderer becomes momentarily satisfied by a desire to inflict damage on other people. During this time, the killer goes through the cooling-off phase. Researchers in the field of criminal psychology have posited that their reason for engaging in violent behavior is the pursuit of a personal pleasure that can only be attained via the employment of abusive behavior. When they murder, these kinds of individuals get a feeling that is equal parts control and empowerment at the same time.

They feel so fulfilled as a result of the experience that they want for the opportunity to rediscover a sense of liberation and pleasure. During the course of their executions, victims were subjected to sexual harassment and torture, as well as humiliation and fear. In addition to hate and anger, additional motivations include obtaining attention, finding delight, and gaining financial reward. Serial killers exhibit predictable patterns in the selection of hostages, the means by which they execute their victims, and the procedures by which they dispose of the bodies of their victims. Researchers that specialize in studying criminal behavior come to the conclusion that individuals who commit serial murders have considerable mental, behavioral, and social disorders.

Even if their crimes do not add up to a cumulative total, it seems as if those who commit serial murders are loners who have difficulties finding suitable romantic partners.

What Is NLP And How Does It Work?

Neuro-Linguistic Programming (NLP) is a branch of research that deals to the interaction of the fundamental aspects of an individual's being that are required in order to produce the human experience. This is necessary in order to produce the human experience. These three facets—neurology, language, and programming—are where Bandler and Grinder got the inspiration for the name of their concept.

The way in which our brain processes the information that it has obtained is the responsibility of the nervous system. Language encompasses, but is not limited to, the process of communication, the manner in which we connect with other people, as well as the means by which we transmit and acquire knowledge. On the other hand, programming is a term that refers to patterns of thinking, as well as an individual's behavior towards learning, and how he uses them in his day-to-day life. Given these breakdowns for an in-depth analysis of what NLP actually is, we could draw the conclusion that the founders of this school of thought intended to assist an individual in developing his total personality, as the expansion of an individual's learning capacity involves not only his intellect but also his entire being.

Furthermore, NLP is not limited to the development and enhancement of an individual's intellectual capacity; rather, it is also a venue for self-discovery, which may refer to how an individual evaluates his capabilities and strives to how he might overcome his weaknesses and shortcomings as he discovers his own liabilities. NLP is a venue for self-discovery. It is also engaged in the finding of the values that a man ought to possess, such as an appetite for the growth of one's spirituality, emotional stability, and a profound sense of humanity, to mention a few. Not just the intellectual component of being human is improved upon, which is one of the many things that makes this school of thinking so admirable, but also the growth of the human being themselves. In their research, Drs. Paul Tosey and Jane Mathison from the School of Management at the University of Surrey noted that NLP, a novel approach to education, has been recognized for its contribution to the growth of both communication and personality. NLP has been referred to as both "an art of communication excellence" and the "study of the structure of subjective experience" due to the all-encompassing nature of the learning approach that it is. In addition, Tosey and Mathison said that NLP was designed to build means to understand how people take part in the processing of information and how they carry out their newly gained knowledge in order for them to achieve their objectives in life. NLP was established in order to construct ways to comprehend how people take part in the processing of information.

NLP, or neuro-linguistic programming, refers to the way in which we make use of the intellectual component of our existence in order to achieve the objectives that we have established for ourselves in our life.

Now that we have a general understanding of what NLP is, let's go further into the subject by conducting an investigation into how NLP operates on an individual level.

It was claimed in an article that was published on the website holistics-online.com that neuro-linguistic programming (NLP) makes use of self-image and the appropriate attitude in order to bring about change in a particular facet of our life. In light of this, it should be clear that NLP supplies you with a situational analysis in which you are free to participate. For instance, if a person recognizes and admits his liabilities and weaknesses, it is feasible for him to overcome them provided he has the will to change these unfavorable aspects of his life. This is only the case, however, if the person has the desire to alter these unfavorable aspects of his life. But of course, it goes without saying that no endeavor would be deemed effective without the collaboration of the willpower and the efforts of an individual to change what it is that they had desired to improve or grow about themselves as individuals. For instance, there are already a number of websites on the internet that provide directions and pointers for the process of building one's personality. One of these websites is freshinsightcoaching.com. On this website, users of the internet are given a number of scenarios along with the accompanying NLP methods that they may learn and utilize in their everyday lives. As an example, there is a part that instructs individuals on how to successfully lose weight. The website not only offers helpful advice for accomplishing weight reduction, but it also encourages its visitors to reflect on the reasons they have not been able to reduce weight without too much difficulty. The aforementioned illustration provides a fundamental illustration of how NLP works. To begin, a situational analysis must be performed so that the person may participate in activities that have the potential to enhance both the manner in which he sees the environment and the way in which he acts in line to what he has observed.

Since we now have a fundamental understanding of how Neuro-Linguistic Programming works, the next step is to investigate the many strategies it employs, investigate its connection to the human capacity for learning, and put those techniques to use in order to improve our capacity for learning and growth so that we may realize our full potential.

The maximization of income should always be your first priority when selling anything. However, the real numbers that matter, both on the board and in the books, are those that come from sales. It is the process of developing a specialized sales presentation that may appeal to a wide variety of different types of customers. In order to do this, a seller has to be able to pique the attention of the buyer and keep it for the duration of the transaction so that he may convey his thought in an effective manner. However, there is not nearly as much of a focus placed on language and emotion as there should be. In addition to familiarity with the product, expertise in sales methods, and specific revenue goals, one must also possess a certain quality. That is the manner in which the words are presented. It all comes down to a single question: what is the best approach for a salesperson to articulate his opinions in a manner that would persuade the customer? The use of Hypnotic Language Patterns in an efficient manner is where the solution may be found. The primary emphasis of this how-to book is on the twenty hypnotic language patterns that are the most prevalent, effective, and widely used, and which have the potential to convert a salesperson into a successful professional.

What Is Hypnotic Language Patterns Such An Essential Topic?

The skill of hypnotizing a person by entrapping their thoughts and focusing their attention is known as hypnosis. The core of the notion behind Hypnotic Language Patterns is the same. They are the words or phrases that, when utilized appropriately, have the potential to elicit the response that a consumer is intended to have. This strategy is entirely predicated on the individual's reaction to the many grammatical structures that might be used to compose a phrase. During this stage of the process, the goal is to communicate a message that has the same meaning but in a manner that is more deft and believable. When a seller gets the hang of starting to communicate his concept in a way that keeps the buyer interested, the remainder of the process doesn't need nearly as much effort on his or her part.

What you should be aware of before starting: Before beginning to comprehend the twenty language patterns that are aimed to elicit an appropriate reaction to a proposal as expressed by the buyer, there are a few pointers that you should be aware of. These suggestions should be kept in mind before beginning to grasp the language patterns. When reading the subsequent chapters of this book, it is essential that these suggestions be kept in mind at all times.

To begin, you shouldn't try it out on random people since it won't provide the outcomes you want. It is essential that you be aware hypnosis does not involve magic. It is a process that has been organized and requires previous engagement as well as a degree of confidence from both persons involved. 2) In the second place, be sure you aren't abusing the method. Because the application of this approach in an inappropriate manner has the potential to inflict significant harm, it must be used only in the manner that is most suited to the current circumstances.3) Thirdly, make things as basic as possible. Any attempt to make a problem more difficult or to hasten its resolution will only serve to make things worse. This method requires one to have both patience and a level head in order to be successful.

A comprehension of what constitutes omissions, generalizations, and distortions

Taking note of a person's meta-programs, values, beliefs, choices, and memories will be very helpful when seeking to comprehend how that person filters incoming information.

It's possible that the word "meta-program" is completely foreign to you. First, consider a program to be a kind of strategy. People have a tendency, during the course of their lives, to acquire coping mechanisms that consist of habitual responses to various aspects of their external environment in which they find themselves.

Take, for example, the concept that is referred to as sorting styles. A person could organize their memories according to the dates of significant events in their lives, the clothes they were wearing, the place they were living, or even the person they were married to or dating at the time. Someone else could choose to describe a thing or event by pointing out how it is similar to or different from something else. Some people sort by concentrating mostly on themselves, while others do it by looking outside. Only a few instances of meta-programs have been shown here. In case you were wondering, "meta" is Greek for "beyond."

In the field of neuro-linguistic programming (NLP), the term "meta-program" refers to a method that seems to permeate a range of contextual actions. The sophisticated language patterns identified by Erickson served as the basis for the development of the NLP meta-programs.

Additionally crucial are one's views and values as a filtering mechanism. A person's values act as a filter, expressing what they consider to be most essential in life. A person is said to have a belief when they are in a psychological state in which they regard a proposition or premise to be true. When a person is exposed to an external event, their value and belief filters cause them to form an internal representation of the event, as well as a state and behavior in response to the event.

For example, if I see an act of kindness or cruelty, the value filters in my brain will produce a certain physiological condition, which in turn may prompt me to do some kind of action. On the other hand, if I watch something being thrown off of a high building, my believing expectancies will lead me to anticipate that the item will hit the ground. Obviously, if it floats instead, I may feel some pain for a short period of time before my mental filters readjust themselves to account for the new reality.

Please be aware of the fact that the words believe and thought or thinking are often confused by those who use them in a sloppy and careless manner. To reiterate, a belief is a mental state that is tied to a presumption of the truth. As a result, I don't just think but rather believe that the ball will fall when it's dropped.

Thinking and thinking relate to a process in which a pattern or shape is generated without relying on perception in any way. Thinking and thinking are synonymous terms. Belief filters may have an effect either a priori or post on thought formation, which is also known as thinking. Belief filters can act either before or after the thought is formed. However, a person with a sufficient level of education should be aware that the two concepts are not even remotely comparable. Despite this, a clinical patient will often be seen confusing one of the two notions with the other.

The sole reason I'm bringing this up is to underline that in NLP, the practitioner often concentrates on altering a subject's thinking process rather than trying to change their beliefs. This is because changing a subject's thought process is easier than changing their beliefs. Changing one's perspective on a belief might, of course, be an effective therapeutic technique. It is essential for the operator to have a clear understanding of whether they want to change the state of the process or the state itself. In most cases, the most effective method for changing a dysfunctional state (or belief system) is to convince the individual to modify their processes by encouraging them to think in a new manner. One of the primary objectives of NLP is to achieve this.

Here Are Some Illustrations Of Hypnotic Language Patterns That You Can Start Using Today!

I'd want to express my gratitude to you for bearing with me while I provided some background knowledge on presuppositions and Hypnotic Language Patterns. Now that we've gone over everything that's important for you to know, let's get right down to business and look at some instances.

The majority of these examples will be centered on making sales, but you'll quickly be able to realize how simple it is to apply these examples to almost any circumstance that comes to mind!

Aspects of Quantity

The following are examples of quantifiers: None, each, every, all, each, every, some, many, and none

The audience is allowed to draw their own conclusions on the precise amount of something after quantifiers have been employed to describe a nebulous quantity. Quantifiers rely on presumptions because they provide the impression that the object in question already exists.

1.) Because it is crafted from genuine wood, my product is a favorite of many of my clients.

Take note of how "Made of real oak" is shown prominently rather than "my customers."

Therefore, the audience's subconcious mind is led to believe that this nebulous "group of customers" is a valid assumption. People who read or listen to what you have to say will automatically assume that you have a significant number of customers. The fact that we utilize our subconcious minds to instinctively fill in quantifiers with anything that has significance to us is one of the factors that contributes to the potency of these expressions. The audience will often assume that your client base is comprised of individuals that are similar to themselves, which is precisely what you want them to do.

2.) My product is so versatile that some of my clients even use it to adorn their coffee tables.

3.) Each and every one of my clients has discovered a wide variety of applications for my product.

4.) Very few of my clients haven't discovered many applications for my product.

The fact that this illustration leans toward the negative makes it more difficult to understand. This is a really captivating sentence, and it will simply fuzze right into the head of the reader. The statement assumes that there is a vast consumer base, and it is expected that the audience will begin to picture all of the other ways in which your product might be used, in addition to its primary and most apparent use. Because of this, each individual will picture something unique, something that is beneficial and significant to them specifically. This gives the idea a great deal of strength. Just right!

Developing Anchors That Are Both Powerful And Beneficial

It may be quite effective to have an understanding of how to develop and use anchors as a means of overcoming negative emotional and behavioral patterns and habits. It's almost as if we're going to make a button that, when hit at any moment, will produce a certain feeling that we've already decided upon. For instance, a person who recognizes that they have a propensity to get too anxious may be able to develop an anchor for a sense of tranquility in themselves. An individual who has a history of rapidly becoming unreasonable and combative in the face of hardship may find it helpful to construct an anchor in order to impart patience and promote critical analysis of the situation.

In most cases, the procedure of developing an anchor involves the use of an uncomplicated physical cue that has the capacity to be triggered or reproduced in the vast majority of contexts with a minimum of difficulty. For instance, many people who are trained in NLP build anchors by tapping their thumb and index finger together in a succession of different patterns. A simple touch on the shoulder from a therapist may help build an anchor of peace for their patients. Athletes may develop anchors for emotions of confidence and attention by utilizing a particular phrase that can be repeated or shouted aloud while they are competing in order to enhance their performance throughout the times of the competition when it is most difficult to find.

Two primary requirements need to be satisfied in order for an anchor to be considered effective. In the first place, it ought to be an unusual provocation, one that is not encountered on a regular basis in regular life. This allows the novelty of the anchor to be preserved while also making it abundantly plain to your mind that the occurrence of the anchor is a trigger to a certain condition. This is the reason why a sequence of taps between the thumb and index finger are employed so often; it is a basic gesture that is very unlikely to be a regular part of your life. In addition, this meets the second condition, which states that the stimulus must be able to be recreated with relative ease in the majority of situations. Because of its intricacy and the high probability that it cannot be replicated under typical conditions, a twenty-second dance performance would make a very unsatisfactory anchor. In the same vein, yelling out a word three times while yelling it loudly would be an awful anchor, supposing that your employer reacts negatively to actions of this kind.

After gaining an understanding of the characteristics of a powerful anchor, the next issue that has to be answered is how we can really establish that anchor.

The procedure starts out with these three components. First, double check that you have chosen the anchor you plan to use. Second, make sure that you have a crystal clear understanding of the desirable mental state that this anchor should induce in you, whether that be serenity, happiness, concentration, self-appreciation, enthusiasm, etc. Third, think back on a time in your life when you felt a certain feeling to its fullest extent and choose an incident from that time to use as an example. If you want to construct an anchor for happiness, you should think back to a time in your life when you were smiling so widely that it pained your cheeks. This is the moment you should choose to use as your anchor.

In order to successfully program this anchor, you need to ensure that you are in what is known as a pure access state. Imagine that this is the sherbet that is served in between the courses of a gourmet dinner, or the coffee beans that are used to clean your nose in between the many scents that you inhale. It is vital to be in a condition devoid of competing emotions in order for us to be able to access the most potent and unadulterated form of the emotional state that we are attempting to replicate. It is quite doubtful that pausing in order to construct an anchor for happiness in the aftermath of a heartbreaking breakup would provide fruitful outcomes.

While you are seated in your pure access state, you will shut your eyes and begin to vividly remember the event that you have selected to identify with your anchor. This will continue until you have completed the process. The buildup has to encompass every imaginable detail, and your absorption in the reenactment needs to be total and convincing for the audience to care. Feel, see, hear, smell, and taste every potential sense, and allow yourself to be open to the range of feelings you had at that moment. Magnify whatever that you can in order to produce an even more powerful condition if at all feasible.

Give your body the chance to respond physiologically. If you want to be an anchor for happiness, give yourself permission to grin from ear to ear without holding back. If you are able to anchor your concentration, you should feel a slowing of your pulse rate. If you are anchoring energy, you should start to feel a pulse of adrenaline in your body. Continue working up to your peak emotional state with as much intensity as you can manage until you reach the pinnacle of your emotional experience. Then, at the precise moment when you have arrived at the pinnacle of this experience, you should present your anchor. You may anchor this state by either saying the trigger word, touching your thumb and index finger together quickly, or doing whatever other action you've decided to take in order to accomplish this. Become aware of how your mind is connecting the event to the anchor. Take it in stride. Then, bring yourself back to a normal condition.

It is possible that the anchor will grab hold of you right away, but this will depend on how well you pushed yourself up to a peak emotional state. It is possible that numerous iterations will be necessary in order to successfully establish the anchor. When you are able to execute the anchor from your baseline condition and conjure up the emotions you experienced at your peak, you will know that you have it. Do not get disheartened if you discover that this is tough for you; it is possible that it is only a question of time and practice.

Ignoring Unfavorable Events And Experiences

Just for a moment, picture yourself tucked away in one of the room's nooks. Imagine that while you read this you can smell the pavement, as if it were covered in moss, and feel the wetness of the cold cobblestone. This sensation is so intense that you can even taste the pavement, as if it were coated in ice. The sound of water dripping very slowly can be heard out in the distance, and it seems as if there is a pipe that is dripping someplace in the shadows. The light goes off completely out of the blue. There is absolutely nothing visible. However, you can now hear footsteps coming closer. You are aware that there is a person standing quite close to you. You get the sensation that someone is tying a rope around both of your hands, and they are also using the rope to bind you to the chair you are sitting in. The next thing you know, you get the impression that something is creeping up the back of your neck. It has the sensation of a large spider.

What emotions did you have as a result of all that happened? Do you agree that it was a little bit awkward? On the other hand, you are aware by this point that you have returned to your cozy seat and are now reading this. You are not in any danger, but for some reason, the thought of that pretty terrifying situation really occurring to you gives you the chills.

The same holds true for your deepest, most irrational dread. You reach a point when you are positive that you have experienced the precise reason why you would always fear being put in an experience that is comparable to the one you just went through. Do you recall the circumstances in which you first met that fear?

When it comes to exercising control, here are some things you should bear in mind: You are influenced to some degree by almost everything that is in your environment; nevertheless, the only thing you can control is how you respond to those influences. That indicates that you are in complete command of both your mental processes and your emotions. That also implies that the greatest method to make the best choices in life is to always have reins over what you believe and what you feel. This is the best approach to make the finest decisions.

Things That Should Be Behind You by Now

When you want to make sure that you are getting what you want out of this life, there are two things that you should learn how to get rid of: harmful suggestion and fear. Learning how to do this will allow you to make sure that you are getting what you want out of this life. What may be the reason behind that? Because the negativity that you believe exists is not actual, but rather a manifestation of something that you can always get rid of, and because of this, the negativity that you think exists is not genuine.

You may want to consider the negative comments that others have made about you throughout your life. It's possible that in the past, someone called you ugly or obese, and since he said it often enough, the voice of that person remains ingrained in your brain to this day. One way or another, there is a memory that everyone would want to just get rid of completely. If they are unable to achieve that, then they will want to make sure that it is no longer something that bothers them.

Separation from one another

You are attempting to get away from the past, which includes things like the negative impression that you have about your surroundings, which is part of the past. You are concerned about the possibility of a similar unfortunate occurrence taking place again. On the other hand, you are aware that by continuing to live with your fear and all of the hurtful things that have been said to you in the past, you are contributing to something that you would very much prefer to steer clear of.

Do not misunderstand - there may be moments when even your decision making will be filled with the worst ideas or feelings, but despite this, you will still be able to get at the conclusion that you want to arrive at. Do not get this confused. On the other hand, if you feel that an event from the past is a reliable source of knowledge for all of the activities that you will be engaging in in the future, you may be in for a rude awakening. Even if the experience has the potential to mold you, much of how it does so depends on how you choose to understand it.

People have a tendency to act in this manner because it is normal for them to do so: they internalize their phobias and terrible experiences to such an extent that they become feelings that they identify with various things and situations in their surroundings. They do it in such a manner that it serves as a warning about the agony or defeat that they would face if they touched or entered them, and as a result, they do not want to contact or enter them. However, they may not even know for certain whether or not these things or situations will genuinely do them harm. They are just making assumptions. Surely, there are times when you act the same way as these other individuals.

However, the NLP method known as dissociation may assist you in reducing the intensity of the feelings that you continue to feel by associating them with the terrible experiences you have had in the past. That implies that if you feel agitated or traumatized after hearing a certain phrase or seeing a specific object, you would be able to take control of those unpleasant feelings and make yourself feel otherwise.

Trying to Get Rid of Negative Thoughts

What causes it to be like that? The reason for this is because individuals arc able to picture in their minds the specific circumstances under which they have felt dread or anguish, and they make an effort to picture those circumstances as well as they can whenever they believe that they are in a situation that is comparable to those circumstances. They are observing the setting as if it were a photograph scaled to real life.

Nevertheless, you may respond in a variety of ways. You may put yourself in similar circumstance, but this time try to see it from a third person point of view, as if you were watching a television show about yourself. Remove all of the color from what you are now seeing. It seems like it happened a long time ago now. The television is then shrunk down to the size of a loaf of bread, however the scene retains its lack of color despite this change. After that, you should continue to reduce its size until it is about the same proportion as a breadcrumb. Since you are unable to see what is currently on the scene, you should simply brush it off.

The Skill Of Influencing One's Own Behavior Via The Use Of Neurolinguistic Processing, Often Known As Nlp

The bulk of this book has been devoted to detailing how to read other people, how to use their emotions and actions against them using a variety of dark psychological tactics, and how to prevent yourself from the same thing occurring to you as it has been discussed in this book. However, what if the individual you needed to perform dark psychology on was...you? When you use neuro-linguistic programming, that is precisely what takes place.

Neuro-linguistic programming, often known as NLP, is a method of psychological manipulation that may be used to create objectives and program yourself to accomplish them; to push you to look at your ideas and values and modify them if required; and to enhance your self-esteem and self-confidence levels. Let's take a look at the background of NLP as well as the practice itself, as well as the ways in which you may make use of it to develop into a more powerful and self-assured individual who is able to create and achieve objectives.

Where It All Began: The Beginnings of Neuro-linguistic Programming

Richard Bandler, a psychologist, and John Grinder, a linguist, were the two Americans responsible for developing NLP in the 1970s. The idea was somewhat inspired by gestalt therapy as well as the earlier research conducted by a psychotherapist and counselor by the name of Virginia Satir. Bandler was also an accomplished computer programmer, and he and Grinder used their combined areas of knowledge to come up with an idea that humans, like computers, could be programmed to behave in a certain manner. This theory was known as the behavioral programming hypothesis.

NLP was the result of Bandler and Grinder's collaboration on a project in which they examined the behaviors and thinking patterns of individuals who were deemed to be extremely successful at that time period. This study culminated in the development of NLP. The guys hypothesized that they might assist individuals program themselves for success if they could identify similarities shared by successful people and devise a mechanism to simulate those shared characteristics.

Beliefs and emotions have a significant role in the development of neuro-linguistic programming. The folks who came up with the idea recognized that in order to be successful, they would not only need to be able to provide other people a very particular formula for success, but they would also need to be able to give that formula to people who think that it is effective.

In more recent years, neuro-linguistic programming (NLP) has been relegated to the status of a pseudo-science; however, for the thousands upon thousands of people who have been using it since its inception and in the years since, it has been a useful tool to increase self-esteem, find the power of positive thinking, set and achieve goals, and change personal beliefs and values. Let's go into the specifics, and then you can make up your own mind about whether or not you want to give it a shot.

The 5 Keys ToNLP Success

More than forty years have passed since the introduction of neuro-linguistic programming. The fact that something has been around for such a long time and continues to be employed in the routine activities of a great number of people suggests that there must be some truth to it, right? We see it being utilized to such a large extent on a commercial basis, and there is no doubt that it has an effect.

Additionally, it has a position in the field of psychology, namely in the field of dark psychology. It is difficult to offer actual evidence of its performance since it is extremely unstructured, and this makes it tough to measure. In addition to this, there is a multitude of unique concepts and strategies for carrying out NLP. It is a sort of treatment that is quite helpful to certain people and actually assists them in leading more fulfilling lives. It's possible that some people won't get anything from it at all. For these individuals to be able to work through their problems and lead lives that are happier and psychologically healthier, they will need to investigate more conventional forms of therapy.

NLP, or the Art of Kicking Unhealthy Habits

It is certain that you will, at some time in the future, become sick of engaging in the same undesirable pattern of behavior that has been making life more difficult for you. It is really challenging to be someone who is unable to effectively manage their time or who constantly puts things off until later. It's possible that your negative habit is based on anything bodily, like chewing your nails or playing with your hair, and you could discover this. Whatever the case may be, Neuro-Linguistic Programming (NLP) could be able to assist you in some manner.

The loop break is one of the strategies that has shown to be one of the most successful methods for breaking undesirable patterns of behavior. It is a method of controlling your conduct in which you do it by removing potentially destructive feelings from your regular activities. This calls for an incredibly acute awareness of both your bodily responses and your mental processes.

Consider the following unfavorable pattern as an example. It's possible that if you're in a new social situation, you have the habit of chewing on your fingernails. This is absolutely not the kind of conduct that should be encouraged.

The first thing you need to do in order to execute a loop break is to think about how your body responds when you are placed in social circumstances that make you feel uneasy. It's quite unlikely that your hands would just shoot up to your lips like that; more than likely, there will be some buildup. It's possible that you'll start to perspire or feel your heart beating.

The next thing you need to do is give some consideration to the feelings that are triggered by the recollections. You undoubtedly have a story to tell about a moment in the past when you were in a social scenario that didn't go as planned. You are certain that you do not want to go through that agony ever again. You need to have a mental conversation with yourself in order to get rid of these negative feelings. Demonstrate to your body how aware you are, and show it that biting is nothing more than a habit that you are able to change.

Having a Weight Loss

Neuro-Linguistic Programming does not inherently promote weight loss; nevertheless, it may help you get in the appropriate frame of mind in order to modify your poor eating and exercise habits so that you might lose weight.

Your first objective should be to improve the perceived attractiveness of nutritious meals. Although it is simple to see why the majority of people would choose a chocolate bar over an apple for a snack, this is not the way to lose weight and should be avoided at all costs.

Your first task is to reevaluate how you now think about the nutritious meals that are readily available to you. At first glance, an apple may not seem like the most appetizing snack option, but your perception can be changed to perceive it in this light. When you look at an apple, you should immediately begin thinking of complimentary words to use to describe it.

You Can Get What You Want If You Ask Enough Questions

Before we begin:

Did you know that asking questions may be a very effective method of covertly influencing someone's opinion? People tend to reveal their innermost ideas in response to questions without even realizing it, which makes this kind of argumentation quite effective. When you are aware of what the other person is considering, it is much simpler to influence their thinking in the direction that you want.

The media, namely newscasters and newspapers, are perhaps the most frequent practitioners of this strategy of subliminal persuasion. Think back to one of the most recent news broadcasts that you tuned in to listen to.

It has been announced that Brad and Jolie will adopt a second child. When will they finally have enough players to field a whole baseball team?

Although adopting children is a charitable act, the news station decided not to make any remarks about this topic. Instead, they steered your thoughts in the direction they desired by asking you a question and then waiting for your response.

This strategy is used by many media outlets in order to influence the ideas and views that you have. They influence your thoughts about the tales so that they are in line with what they want you to believe about them. After hearing this, I take it you're not such a big lover of the media anymore?

It would not make a difference even if a news story turned out to be inaccurate, and the source afterwards apologized and retracted the story after admitting their mistake. Your perspective on the situation, whether favorable or unfavorable, has already been established.

Are you beginning to see the significance of the role that questions play in the NLP persuasive technique?

Are you prepared to begin using questions as a means of swaying people's opinions?

It is simple to manipulate the course of a discussion by asking questions at the appropriate places. You only need to mention whatever it is that you want people to be considering once you've presented it to them. For instance, you may say something like, "I agree, you want to spend the holidays on the cabin by the lake, just like we have for the last five years." But can you imagine how much more thrilling it would be for the two of us to go on a journey to a completely new area together for the very first time?

You may influence the outcome of a variety of different scenarios by using questions in this manner.

Presuppositions Made by NLP

In the field of neuro-linguistic programming (NLP), presuppositions are fundamental generalizations or broad assumptions that might be helpful to you if you behave as if they are true.

The following are some presumptions that are often made in NLP:

1. The Statement "The Map Is Not the Territory" Belongs to Alfred Korzybski, Who Gets the Credit for It. He argues that the human senses of sight, touch, hearing, taste, and smell are what allow us to perceive the world, which he refers to as 'the territory.' The information that you get from your encounters with these senses is then transported to the brain, where it is processed and used to create an internal representation that he refers to as "the map."

Your life experiences help to build the internal map that you develop in your brain, but even someone who has had the exact same life experiences as you will never have an internal map that is an identical replica of yours (this is because other people's perceptions and the way their senses receive information may be different). What this essentially implies is that the world outside and the world within your head can never be the same thing at the same time.

It's possible that, as a medical professional, your understanding of what pills are and what they accomplish is drastically distinct from that of a patient or even a law enforcement officer. The idea is that each of us forms unique mental representations of the same objects, based on our individual histories and the circumstances in which we find ourselves.

You need to learn how to view things through the perspective of other people in order to be a better communicator and a better person in general. To do this, you need make an effort to comprehend the internal representations or map of the person with whom you are attempting to communicate. Focus on attempting to understand why the other person would have acted in such a manner rather than giving a negative reaction to conduct that you may believe to be unacceptable on the part of other individuals. Because of this, you will become a happy person who is able to accept the acts and inactions of other people with more ease.

2. There is no such thing as failure; only feedback is provided: You will benefit from this extremely fundamental NLP premise, but only if you are able to adhere to it in your daily life. There is not a single individual in this whole globe who does not at some point or another fall short of their goals. It is up to you to decide whether you will let those failures bring you down or if you will draw lessons from those failures and use these lessons as learning experiences that will help you become better at whatever it was that you failed at the first time when you decide to attempt it again.

In the event that you are unsuccessful at anything, rather than giving up, constantly ask yourself the following five questions:

* "What is it that I'm trying to accomplish?"

* "What have I been able to accomplish up until this point?"

* "What are the things that I have learned from this experience (feedback)?"

* "How can I better apply the knowledge I've gained to improve my performance?"

* "How am I going to measure both my performance and my success?"

3. The Response that the communication generates is the Meaning of the Communication: The way in which the individual you are speaking with understands the information that you are attempting to convey to them is the single most significant factor. Your listener will construct an interpretation of the material depending on how they take in the information, regardless of how excellent your intentions are.

The responsibility for conveying your words to your audience in the manner in which you would want them to be received falls squarely on your shoulders. Before beginning to communicate, make sure that you have a crystal clear grasp of the conclusion that you want the discussion to have, and then carefully arrange your communication in a way that will elicit the reaction that you are looking for.

4: If What You Are Doing Is Not Working, Do Something Different: This is yet another assumption, and it is a pretty basic one at that. If what you are doing isn't working, try something else. Instead of becoming dogmatic about strategies that aren't producing results for you, try switching things around.

Try to figure out why the things you are doing are not producing the desired outcomes and what changes you might do to improve things.

5. You have all the Resources You Need to Create the Outcomes You want: Everyone has what it takes to develop, grow, and become a better version of themselves. If you want to create the outcomes you want, you need to believe that you have all the resources you need.

6. People are Much More than Their Behavior People are much more than their behavior; the fact that someone is acting poorly does not always suggest that they are horrible as a person. When people lack the resources inside themselves to conduct in a different manner, they exhibit poor behavior. The vast majority of the time, assisting them in modifying or bettering these resources would help them alter their behavior and begin acting in a more positive manner.

7: The Importance of Your Body Language: Because body language accounts for 55% of how people understand what you are saying, it is imperative that you utilize appropriate body language whenever you are speaking with others.

You will need to put the strategies in this book into practice for them to be effective for you. The majority of these methods are not quick fixes that are going to work in a single day; but, with regular practice, your life would improve, and you would become better at whatever it is that you want to get better at.

In the chapters that follow, we will go through how to use various NLP strategies to achieve a variety of different objectives. First things first, let's establish some personal moorings.

How To Apply NLP In Your Everyday Life

In order to make use of NLP in your everyday life, there are a few procedures that you will need to take. The following are the measures that need to be taken to adopt.

Take note

Initially, you should consider monitoring your present behavior. Examine the ways in which you react to the many stimuli that are present around you. How good is your ability to converse with other people? How can you make sense of the things that are going on around you? What do you believe the general consensus of others is towards you? You are obligated to locate the appropriate answers to each of these questions and record them. When you are assessing your development in the future, you will go back to them for guidance.

Compare with

The next thing you need to do is encourage other people to see how you conduct yourself. It has already been established that not everyone has the same way of thinking, and it is inevitable that people will continue to have divergent points of view. You need to have someone write down bits of your conduct both at home and at work, and that someone may be either a coworker or a friend. Gather their feedback and evaluate it in light of the information you have put down. This will help you determine whether or not you are really behaving the way you believe you are, or whether or not it is significantly different from how other people see you. Establish your objectives.

The next step is to develop some attainable objectives for yourself that you want to pursue. Your ability to communicate, listen, and offer your points of view in a more effective manner should all improve as a result of achieving these objectives. Your overall growth as a person will be accelerated as a direct result of your efforts in each of these areas.

Get moving on it!

The next step is to design a strategy that will assist you in achieving the objectives that you have established. Because making plans is relatively simple to execute, but really putting those ideas into action is often where people struggle, this may be the most critical step here. You have to identify the areas in which you are making mistakes and then correct them. On the other hand, if you are succeeding at something, you need to continue doing what you are doing. For instance, if you are strong at beginning conversations, you should work on improving your habit by learning how to continue the discussion in a more effective manner. On the other side, if you have a reputation for being a poor listener, you should make it a point to cultivate the practice of listening attentively.

Consider in detail.

After you have begun working toward your objectives, you should examine your progress on a regular basis to determine whether or not you are on the right path. On the one side, you need to have a plan of action, and on the other, you need to gauge how far along you are. It is imperative that you examine whether or not you are actively working toward changing who you are and welcoming the new you with open arms.

When you reach the point when you believe you have accomplished what you set out to do, you are free to go on to another objective, and so on.

In reality, achieving this goal is a great deal easier than it would first seem. When it comes to making a connection with a potential customer, nothing beats echoing back to them their most important phrases and the things they believe. First, let's review some essential vocabulary. In the second phase, you interrogated the potential customer. You will notice that your prospect will repeat certain words or phrases over and over again. Your potential customer will emphasize their significance to him whenever the aforementioned terms and phrases are brought up in discussion with you. The issue that has to be answered is how does he achieve it? What does he mean when he says that these words are so significant? According to a popular proverb, "everyone is different;" yet, in this scenario, everyone places an emphasis on the phrases that are significant to them. When a prospect wants to emphasize a word or phrase, I can usually tell because they will lean forward while doing so. This is the method that I find to be the most reliable. When someone is thinking about something for a little period of time, their eyes may often seem to have a glassy appearance. On occasion, I have also seen people gripping their fists or hands when they are at tables. Some persons have a slouched posture. You won't have any trouble recognizing it at all. When you are next in a public place, observe how two individuals interact with one another while they are talking. You're going to notice that some words or phrases cause an emotional response in others. They will generally emphasize particular words or phrases by leaning in closer.

Those of you who do your business over the phone will be able to immediately hear the emphasis that is placed on the words. You'll hear specific phrases that are repeated stretched out or in a different tone each time they come up. If you pay attention to it, you will undoubtedly discover it.

Permit me to illustrate with an example. A while ago, I had a prospect who was considering purchasing insurance via the firm that I worked for. They expressed interest in doing so to me. Our rates were far higher than those of her previous employer. After establishing a good relationship with her, I started asking her some questions, such as, "Why did you decide to go with that particular insurance company?" What is it about them that appeals to you? What is it about this particular day that prompted you to contact us?"

The topic of "security" was brought up many times over the course of the discussion. My whole interaction took place over the phone, but even from that distance, I could see that the lady desired safety. She used the word "security" in the same way that some people use the word "chocolate." You could almost sense the need that she had for this so-called "security." Now bear in mind that I had no notion what this lady meant by the concept of security. Everyone has a distinct conception of what constitutes safety. The only thing I needed to do to complete the deal with her, despite the fact that our pricing was $300 more per year than theirs, was to tell her how much "security" she would feel working with us. I made it clear that I thought it was "Great! This other firm won't be able to provide you the same level of safety that this one will, but this one certainly can. Let's get this insurance up and running now so that you may experience that sense of safety right away.

NLP Benefits

You are the Chief Executive Officer of Your Experience.

What results do you get when you put restrictions on yourself? Are you conscious of the fact that you do it? It's possible that without even realizing it, you've spent your whole life cultivating ideas that restrict your potential in ways that you aren't even aware of. You may, on some level, believe that other people are more successful, more attractive, or more deserving of affection than you are on your own. You may convince yourself via your regularly scheduled mental programming that you will never be better than someone else at XYZ, thus there is no use in attempting to become better at it.

You are not required to really conduct your life in such a manner, which is a huge relief. With the help of NLP, you will be able to alter all of those self-fulfilling prophesies and limiting assumptions about who you are and what you contribute to the world. You will be able to discover how to modify your negative thinking patterns after you have begun to study and comprehend the thought processes that lead you to feel that you are not worthy or that you do not deserve to be successful. The larger picture is that all of the limiting ideas that you say, think, and feel are contained inside the thought patterns in your mind that you operate like computer programs. You may finally start living the life you've always dreamed of after you educate yourself how to run new thoughts and mental processes, as well as how to train yourself more constructive communication and skills for regulating your internal state.

One of the numerous advantages of engaging in this form of training is that it may help you take control of your own thoughts. If you are able to get an understanding of how you act and how you respond to or perceive the environment, you will be able to learn how to modify the aspects of your life that are ineffective or that do not align with your ideal existence. Nobody, other than you, can actually have influence over the thoughts and emotions that you experience. This is a really significant education. As soon as you understand how beneficial that is, you will be moving in the correct direction. Nobody can genuinely bring you pain until they make physical contact with you. You alone have the capacity to form the thought patterns, or modify them, that lead you to have severe or strong emotional responses to ordinary life and the people in it. NLP teaches you how to comprehend this fact and shows you how to put it into practice.

Unless you choose to let it, the state of mind, emotions, or circumstances of others have no bearing on how we respond to the circumstances in which we find ourselves. You may begin to grasp how you are the master of your experience when you learn the methods of NLP, which are explained later in the book. Once you have mastered that, you can:

Develop your ability to communicate with others as well as with yourself.

Improve your own understanding of your motives as well as those of others.

Improve the all-around quality of your life's health.

Reduce and do away with all of your worries, tension, and anxiety.

Make more effective and time-saving blueprints for anything you want to do in your life, then do it.

Gaining a greater degree of behavioral and emotional flexibility will serve you well during times of difficulty.

Have the mental flexibility to guide your life in a direction that is more well-balanced.

It all boils down to the changes you want to make, and if you don't like the way things are going in your life or the way you feel, you are the only one who can alter any of those things. Learn how to shift and reframe old thought patterns and programming that keep you locked in doubt; how to become more attuned to your true self; how to act resourcefully in stressful times; and how to see that we are all living life through our own subjective experiences and can afford each other greater compassion and respect. NLP empowers you to learn how to do all of these things and more.

The Various Forms Of NLP Instruction

When training in Neuro-Linguistic Programming first began, sessions were not only held in groups but also in real time. It was a common assumption that there was a greater probability of comprehension if one thought about another person in person. Because of the proliferation of technology and the internet in this century, an increasing amount of education is being offered online. In addition to this, it is widely acknowledged as an efficient method of learning and instruction.

The opportunity to understand the study material and practice it on a regular basis and at a time that is convenient for oneself is one of the advantages that come with participating in online training. Concerning the NLP training, it is necessary to make certain that it properly aligns with the demands, style, and choice of the individual. Before training can begin, there are a number of elements that need to be examined and reviewed, including the following:

• The financial capabilities • The focused usage and philosophy • The time required to finish the course • The credibility of the training facility • Any endorsements and certification • The assistance one receives while they are being trained

The Methods That Are Employed in NLP

NLP makes use of a variety of different strategies, some of which are as follows:

Put simply, anchoring

This calls for a complete overhaul of the sensory impacts and experiences. After that, when they are provoked, they bring about the emotionally charged circumstance.

Relationship building

They are able to transform into the person by imitating the individual's bodily behaviors; as a result, this helps to improve communication and leads to an increased empathy response.

Patterns with a Swish

It is essential to alter patterns of behavior and make conscious choices about what one wants and does not desire.

Dissociation of the Eyes

Eliminating negative thoughts and any associations with previous events is a necessary step in this process.

NLP Technique: Different Types of Beliefs in NLP

In the field of natural language processing, we investigate the effects of transformations. We are interested in how different beliefs affect us and are willing to investigate and "test" a variety of them in order to determine which of these beliefs is the most convincing and effective.

If we have faith that we are capable of doing something, there is a good chance that we will really carry it through.

If we are under the impression that we are incapable of doing anything, we are more likely to avoid even attempting it, or if we do try it, we will do it with a mindset that is characterized by passivity and lack of willpower.

Why are belief systems and their evolutions considered such an important part of NLP?

Certain convictions get ingrained in one's mind over time, regardless of whether or not these convictions can be supported by evidence derived from the outside world. This is very normal, and even the most ardent skeptics among us hold to this kind of faith. One of the most fascinating aspects about convictions is that we are able to firmly establish them on a more fundamental level. We take it for granted that they are "right," and we aren't even aware of the ways in which they shape our actions. We could even hold them to the point where we would be quite surprised if someone were to question them. This would make us very wutend.

There are two aspects of conviction that need to be taken into consideration: self-confidence and the effects of this conviction.

The act of believing in something or someone is, in most cases, an extension of one's knowledge of that person or thing.

"Presentational speaking has never been one of my strong suits."

"The Geschaftsleitung did not pressure me to comply."

"No one from Company X is a good fit for this position."

The effect that a conviction has on our behavior is the implication of that conviction. This effect has an effect on our behavior. I'm willing to consider any and all possibilities, but if something doesn't apply to me or anybody else in this conversation, I don't see how it can be considered relevant to the topic at hand.

It is not necessarily relevant right now whether the things being discussed are true or not; what is more important is the following question: if the things in which I have faith cannot be shown to be true and the people in my immediate environment are negatively affected as a result, why do I continue to have faith in them?

NLP Is An Abbreviation For Neuro-Linguistic Programming.

Neuro-linguistic programming, abbreviated as NLP, is the form of Mind Control that is the most up-to-date and readily available to the general public.

NLP was developed by therapists who were successful in accomplishing their therapeutic aims in a very short amount of time. Not only has it been shown that NLP is an efficient method of treatment, but it is also a very powerful covert tool of both persuasion and manipulation. When a therapist is able to quietly persuade a client to adopt a new solution to their difficulty, that therapist is then in a position to utilize the same strategies to promote a product or even infuse a new credo list into the individual.

In the same way that NLP is a science, this is also an art, and in order to master it, one has to have a solid grasp of the NLP model and the procedures that are used in it, as well as the time to practice it.

In order to fully comprehend the NLP model, the first step is to acknowledge the various ways in which individuals are similar to and distinct from one another. Because there are only a limited amount of ways for us to understand our own experiences, we are all the same. We are unique in that each individual has his or her own distinctive method of making sense of the things that have happened to them. You need to modify their message so that it is appropriate for the individual who is aware of how everyone else makes sense of their reality, and it ought to be accepted.

It should come as no surprise that it has been taken up and exploited in the sectors of sales and advertising, as well as in the area of assisting people in getting laid, using the power that is stated in NLP.

Sensitivity of the senses The term "Pay Attention!" is referred to in the NLP jargon as "Sensory Acuity."

It essentially implies that you need to pay more attention to how they respond while interacting with other people rather than focusing on whether or not you are doing things correctly. People will respond to you in very understated ways when you do that ("Pay Attention!"), as you will discover when you do that.

Finding the person you want to be with is just one aspect of what constitutes a healthy relationship. It is quite conceivable for someone to like you while also maintaining a friendship with someone else. The fact that the other person sees you as being very similar to them on a fundamental level is crucial to the success of any romantic relationship.

This makes the person feel more at ease with you and prepares them to respond to you with a feeling of acceptance and relaxation. (Yes, despite the fact that they dislike you, they will still show consideration for you. Imagine two competitors who secretly care for one another.) It has been stated, and it is absolutely true, that nothing is conceivable without any connection, but that with any relationship, everything is possible.

When it comes to developing relationships, the first lessons often taught are "mirroring" and "matching" behaviors.

The term "mirroring" refers to the practice of genuinely behaving and speaking in a manner that is similar to that of the other person, while doing so in a way that does not seem to be mimicking. This gives the other person the illusion that you are similar to them, even if it's not intentional.

People who are already in relationships automatically reflect one another, and this is something that can be seen. When one of them shifts position, the other adjusts his sitting arrangement to mirror the new orientation of the first person. Developing some kind of romantic connection is a fairly normal next step.

The participants in many NLP trainings engage in mirroring and matching exercises for extended periods of time in order to learn how to more easily create connections. The exercises are really beneficial; nevertheless, there is a more straightforward approach.

Instead than considering mirroring to be the origin of the connection, which is the more common approach, it is a more effective technique to gain partnerships. In other words, if you admire someone and have the impression that you are similar to that person, you will naturally form a romantic connection with that person and copy and match their behaviors without even realizing it. You just need to convince yourself that you're the same as this other person. Imagine that the connection already exists and that you and the other person have a substantial familiarity with the inner thoughts and outward actions of the other person. It may need some mental gymnastics at first, but it is far simpler than paying close attention to how other people are moving and then attempting to move one's body in a way that is similar to what other people are doing.

Principal Forms And Methods Of Manipulation

As a result of the fact that the method of manipulation often varies according to who is being manipulated or where the manipulator is located, there are several forms of manipulation. For instance, some manipulators concentrate on workplace methods while others will utilize their manipulative skills regardless of where they are or who they are with. Both types of manipulators are considered to be manipulators.

Emotional Manipulation Done in Secret

Any kind of manipulation may include some degree of covert manipulation of the target's emotions. On the other hand, it is more prevalent among persons who are known as "master manipulators" or those who would influence anybody in order to achieve everything they desire. These people have a greater propensity to engage in manipulative behavior. It is not as effective as a deception method that individuals employ when they tell someone else that they are alright, even while something is wrong with them.

The goal of this manipulation, which is referred to as covert emotional manipulation, is to influence the way individuals think and feel, and this is the foundation of the manipulation. In order to exert power over you, they concentrate on your conscious awareness. People don't notice that they're being influenced nearly as much as they should because of this.

First, the manipulator will win your confidence by demonstrating that they can be trusted. After that, they will begin to exert power on your thoughts, feelings, and overall perspective of the world around you. They will go slowly toward their goal because they do not want you to recognize that you are being manipulated. As soon as they get the impression that they have control over your feelings and ideas, they will begin to chip away at your self-assurance. A skilled manipulator is aware that in order to manage you in the manner that they want, they must first bring your self-esteem down. They will also make an effort to strip you of your identity, which will enable them to have complete control over you.

In addition to attempting to tear you down emotionally and psychologically, they will try to isolate you from your loved ones and prevent you from communicating with them. One of the most important reasons for doing this is to stop those who knew you before the new people in your life came into it from approaching you because they see the new people as a danger. Your loved ones and friends will see a change in you, and it won't be a change that they approve of. They will investigate the reason for your shift in behavior and, in most cases, they will point the finger at the manipulator in a very short amount of time. When anything like this occurs, your close friends and family will do all in their power to find out what is being done to you by this person and how you are being treated by them. In intimate relationships, this is one of the most typical indications of manipulative behavior.

Naturally, you will begin to recognize a shift occurring on the inside of yourself. Regrettably, this happens almost always after the manipulator has gained power over you. When you first discover that you are feeling different, you will start to notice that you are changing as well. It's possible that you'll start to experience symptoms such as anxiety, depression, difficulty sleeping, difficulty trusting individuals who you formerly trusted, and a growing sense of isolation ("Covert Emotional Manipulation").

It is difficult for the majority of individuals to recognize the telltale signals of manipulators. This is particularly true for those individuals who are susceptible to being manipulated by the person they are romantically involved with. In general, it might be difficult to recognize certain indicators of manipulation. In addition, it is sometimes more difficult to recognize these behaviors in individuals whom you love and who you feel love you in return. In romantic partnerships, individuals often "turn a blind eye" to the manipulative behaviors of their significant other because they consider such behaviors to represent flaws in themselves. When we are in partnerships, we make an effort to comprehend the shortcomings of one another.

When it comes to relationships, there are a lot of different indicators that point to the presence of manipulation, and although you should be aware of the personality qualities of a manipulator, there are also a lot of additional symptoms. This is due to the fact that people who are skilled at manipulation often relax their guard when they are at home. They are operating from a place of ease and confidence, certain that they are capable of doing anything, while you are too helpless to defend yourself or make an effort to alter the situation.

They will provoke you into a battle over something little to get their own advantage.

The urge to win is something that manipulators have, and it shows itself rather often in the relationships they have, particularly romantic connections. Therefore, if you are having a tiny dispute with your significant other, you may notice that they may make it into a battle so that you enable them to win. This is because they want you to let them win. They want you to give up and do whatever it is they want to do to achieve their goals.

They are really good at keeping a secret.

They don't like it when you hide any secret from them, but they can keep everything they want from you. You can't do anything about it. In addition, they are not required to provide you with any information on what they are doing or where they are going. This is irrelevant to you in every possible way. In other words, you should mind your own business and not interfere with what they are doing since it is none of your concern.

However, if you continue to treat them in the same manner, they will either start a quarrel with you, claim that you do not love them, or grow furious with you. This is due to the fact that they will lose control of the situation if they do not have complete information on you. They are also able to maintain power over you despite the fact that you are not privy to any of their secrets.

Their acts and words do not correspond with one another.

The people who manipulate you are aware that in order to maintain their power over you, they will sometimes have to indulge your desires. This may be in the form of presents, but more often than not, they will concentrate on telling you what it is that they think you want to hear. However, they will not stick to their word and complete what they have promised. For instance, if you are experiencing feelings of loneliness and don't want your significant other to continue spending time with their friends, you can request that they spend the night with you. You are going to inquire about some time alone or about going with them. They will provide you with an explanation as to why tonight is not going to work, but they will then promise to spend more time with you or that the two of you will participate in an activity on another evening. Regrettably, they are not very good at keeping their word or keeping their commitment.

They will put on a show of being victimized.

There is never a period when you and your significant other won't quarrel with one another or when you won't strive to defend yourself or your position. This occurs not just at the beginning of the relationship but also all the way through it. When it occurs, the person who is doing the manipulating is going to act like they are the one who is being victimized. They will interpret what you say in such a way as to make it seem as if you are the one acting inappropriately. They will continue to utilize their feelings to try to convince you to believe them, even if it's possible that at first you won't agree with their perspective of the situation.

Sinister Influence And The Art Of Manipulation

Distinction between the Art of Persuasion and That of Manipulation

By using strategies that are both deceitful and underhanded, persons who wish to acquire power or influence over you will often resort to covert emotional manipulation as one of their primary tools. People with this mindset want to subtly alter the way you think and act without ever letting you know that this is what they are doing. In other words, they use methods that might change your views in such a manner that makes you believe that you are acting freely in spite of the fact that they are controlling your actions. The term "covert" refers to the fact that you are not consciously aware of the fact that the manipulation of your emotions is taking place. Those who are skilled in the use of such methods may coerce you into doing what they want you to do even though you are aware of it; they can keep you "psychologically captive."

When talented manipulators set their eyes on you, they may convince you to give them control over your own emotional well-being and even your sense of what you are worth as a person. They will enchant you in such a way that you will be under their control without you recognizing it. They will earn your confidence, and you will begin to place importance on what others think of you as a result of this. After you have let them into your life, they will begin to methodically destroy your entire identity, and as time passes, you will lose your sense of self-worth and become whomever it is that they want you to be.

Once you have invited them into your life, they will begin to do this.

It's probably more prevalent than you'd expect for someone to manipulate others covertly emotionally. People are seldom aware that it is occurring to them because of how subtle it is, and in other situations, they may never even realize that it is happening to them because of how subtle it is. When this kind of manipulation is taking place, it's possible that only acute outside observers will be able to discern.

It's possible that you know someone who was a lot of fun and outgoing in the past, but after becoming involved with another person and waiting a few years, she gives off the impression of having an entirely different personality. If you haven't seen an old buddy in a while, you may not even recognize the person she has evolved into. This exemplifies how effective covert manipulation of an individual's emotions can be. It is possible for someone to undergo a full personality transformation without even being aware of it. The manipulator will gradually chip away at you, and you will accept minute alterations that are difficult to detect, until the old you is replaced by a new version of you that is constructed to be submissive to the manipulator.

Emotional manipulation in the shadows might be compared to a coup d'état in slow motion. It needs you to make little concessions to the person who is attempting to influence you, and you need to make these concessions gradually. In other words, in order to accommodate the manipulative person, you end up giving up little parts of your identity, and as a result, it never occurs to you that there could be a more significant factor at play.

You will give in to the manipulative person's demands to change in seemingly little ways because you don't want to "sweat the small stuff." However, if you begin to give in to the demands of the manipulative individual, a domino effect will begin to take place. You will be more comfortable making future compromises, and your individuality will be wiped and replaced in a cumulative development.

Training And Certificates In NLP Are Available Here

There are two primary certifications available in NLP. Both the Practitioner and the Master Practitioner levels are included here. It has been largely agreed upon by the majority of organizations, the most of which have since ceased operations, that have claimed to be credentialing authority for NLP credentials that each of these programs needed a total of 130 hours of classroom training. The most common method of delivery was in the form of 16 hours spread out over the course of each month, a procedure that would typically take anywhere between eight and nine months to complete. In several of the programs, the students were needed to pass a practical exam, which was also referred to as an integration on occasion.

In this examination, the students were asked to exhibit their abilities. In addition, a written test is necessary for admission to some programs.

There has been a movement in the direction of condensing NLP training courses into full programs that are completed in 10 days or less. In most cases, these are preceded by the reading of a self-study book, which the participant has to finish and then pass an exam on before beginning the preparation for the ten-day marathon.

My official education was completed in the more extensive framework of a two-year course. Even if I may have a bias for that format because of my experience with it, I believe that it is more productive and results in more skilled practitioners. The rationale for this conclusion is because the capacity to witness real-life communication is the source of a significant portion of the integration that occurs between NLP theory and practice. The learner has a greater capacity to absorb and apply the information when it is presented to them over the course of a condensed period of time, such as a weekend that is divided into four eight-hour segments and then followed by a month of homework. Regrettably, many prospective students who would want to advance at a much faster speed may be discouraged from enrolling in this course due to its style. Also, the expedited forms may occasionally be given at a much lesser cost, while yet giving the trainers with a noticeably larger profit.

There is a possibility that some Master Practitioners may be curious in becoming certified teachers. John Overdurf and Julie Silverthorne, who were co-trainers and assistants for

Richard Bandler, were the ones who led the program that I participated in and were responsible for my education. Their curriculum, which I assume is similar to those provided by Bandler and Tad James, entails a highly tough written test, two weeks of intense teacher training, and a week of demonstrations during which the student demonstrates their ability to teach the content. (I feel it necessary to bring out that when I went through the program, all of the information that was provided to me was based upon content that was between thirty and forty years old.)

Persuasion

The capacity to deliver things in such a manner as to convince others to believe the facts or encourage them to make a choice is what we mean when we talk about the skill of persuasion.

Persuasion and influence, as you can see, both require a change in behavior and attitudes, but the distinction between the two lies in the manner in which this change occurs. You are attempting to convince the other person when you make an effort, via your actions and words, to alter the conduct of the other person. Through the use of your personality, you are attempting to exert influence on the other person if you are successful in changing their attitudes and behaviors.

People have a propensity to repay favors that have been done for them. It frequently comes back in good measure, pressing and spilling over, similar to what is mentioned in the Bible about giving. Adam Grant is a professor at the University of Pennsylvania, where he also works as an author and psychologist. He details data in his book titled "Give and Take," which shows that those who consistently aid others are more successful in the long term.

Giving here does not have to take the form of monetary contributions. You might provide your time, guidance, support, or knowledge, among other things. This idea is often shown on the websites of many companies. Let's imagine you're interested in purchasing a product that will help you shed some pounds. You go to one website, which only provides you with a list of their items along with the advantages of using them.

The second page begins by providing you with details on your current weight. It gives you access to a free calculator that you may use to determine your Body Mass Index. It provides an explanation of what your body mass index (BMI) signifies in relation to your weight and your general health. It provides information on the many elements, such as age, lifestyle, nutrition, and so on, that might impact your weight. You are given access to all of this content prior to making even a single financial commitment.

Which online store will you be purchasing from? Which option should you pick? You will bookmark the website so that you may return to it when you are prepared to make a purchase, even if you do not buy anything right away. You should also subscribe to ensure that you are kept up to date with any new information that becomes available.

When you give to others, you provide them with a sense of worth and appreciation. They will be more than willing to reciprocate when you ask anything of them in the future, whether it be to make a purchase or to participate in a certain cause. Giving first and then asking for what you want is a powerful strategy.

When formulating the message you want to send, keep your audience in mind. It is essential that the style in which one speaks to high school pupils and older people be distinct from one another. You could also need to adjust how people of various genders portray themselves.

Let us take the example of health items; more specifically, let us use the example of weight reduction products. When marketing these kinds of items to women, you may underline how important it is for them to have a body that looks beautiful in adorable dresses, prevent stretch marks, and have a bikini physique, among other things. These are concerns that are very near and dear to them.

It's possible that men won't react as positively to a message framed in this way. It seems that the term "fat" does not have the same repulsive connotation for guys as it does for women. What about getting new clothing that are one to three sizes bigger if the previous ones don't fit? And don't even start talking about how beautiful the beach is. They won't give a damn about anybody staring at them as they strut about shirtless and proudly display their beer bellies on their vacation. They make their name seem more intimidating by appending the word "big" to the beginning of it. Thank you very much for your assistance, Big Austin.

See? A message that is well accepted by the women but not by the men is passed in and out of both groups. It's possible that if you strike them where it hurts (figuratively and physically), you can persuade guys to listen to what you have to say. Make a connection between your goods and sexual wellness. To be more specific, sexual prowess. The thought that they can behave like monsters (or anything close to it) in bed may convince them to consume oats and celery sticks much more quickly. Or anything else that you could recommend.

Do not overwhelm a creative person, such as an artist, with an excessive amount of analytical data while you are chatting to them. You should save it for the corporate leaders. These people are obsessed with statistics and insist that numbers don't lie. Creative people become energized when they hear how ideas will be put into action.

Depending on the person you are conversing with, you need to give careful consideration to the particulars that you select to illustrate. These are just a few instances of how the message might be personalized to the individual who will be reading it. The guiding principle applies not just to the realm of business but also to other aspects of life. You should now be able to do the same, depending on the circumstances that you find yourself in.

When people do not immediately favorably accept your message, you must be prepared to speak it again and again until they do. Doesn't it seem like nagging to you? Certainly not in every case. Consider candidates for political office who are making their case to voters. They run their campaign for a number of months, during which time they engage in daily conversations with members of the public and basically reiterate the same message. In the event that they are unsuccessful in winning that specific election, they will run again in the next one and continue to elaborate on the reasons why they think they are in the greatest position to serve the people. Abraham Lincoln, the 16th President of the United States, ran unsuccessfully for office eight times before finally winning the election for president.

There is a certain allure to the kind of guy (or woman) who never stops asking questions. One who does not yield to pressure or intimidation. People are persuaded that he has ideas that will have an effect on their life as a result of his tenacity. Even the most obstinate among them eventually gave up and listened.

How can you be persistent without being annoying to others around you? Continue to rephrase the message in your own words. Change the way you say things. Every time, provide a few more specifics. Create a demonstration or a prototype. Gather all the pertinent data. People are more likely to react positively to anything that can be seen as compared to words alone. Allow the individuals listening some time to consider the facts before continuing the conversation. Keep pounding on that door, and sooner or later, it will open for you in one way or another, no matter what.

You need to speak with conviction if you want other people to perceive things from your perspective. The listener forms their initial impression of you based on your verbal and nonverbal communication, which in turn influences how they feel about you. Confidence is essential whether you are communicating with others, whether it is in front of a large audience, a small group, or just one individual.

How do you let others know that you are confident? First, let's look at body language. Carry yourself with pride as you go. Keep your gaze fixed on the target. Raise and firmly shake both hands. People will become more interested in listening to what you have to say as a result of this. Pay close attention to what the listener has to say when it is their chance to speak. Doze off every so often.

A confident person exudes an air of positive energy that is immediately contagious to everyone around them. It inspires people, and it gets them excited about your ideas. They can see that you are enthusiastic about the concept, which will pique their interest and make them more likely to want to give it a go.

Make it clear to your audience that there is a certain amount of time. The majority of the time, this tactic is used in marketing. What do they say to you, exactly? Be quick, since supplies are limited! This offer is only good for the first one hundred customers! If you buy it now, you may receive a discount! In most of these deals, they will try to make you think that the supply is restricted when, in reality, it is not. They are aware that a feeling of urgency is effective. They are successful in making you believe that being one of the first purchasers and receiving a certain offer would be an honor for you. And it is effective.

Nevertheless, when it comes to topics pertaining to marketing, make sure you demonstrate that other people have showed interest in your ideas or offered positive evaluations of them. In this day and age of social media, you may depend on the reaction you're receiving online as confirmation that there is interest in what you're offering.

Persuasion

The capacity to deliver things in such a manner as to convince others to believe the facts or encourage them to make a choice is what we mean when we talk about the skill of persuasion.

Persuasion and influence, as you can see, both require a change in behavior and attitudes, but the distinction between the two lies in the manner in which this change occurs. You are attempting to convince the other person when you make an effort, via your actions and words, to alter the conduct of the other person. Through the use of your personality, you are attempting to exert influence on the other person if you are successful in changing their attitudes and behaviors.

People have a propensity to repay favors that have been done for them. It frequently comes back in good measure, pressing and spilling over, similar to what is mentioned in the Bible about giving. Adam Grant is a professor at the University of Pennsylvania, where he also works as an author and psychologist. He details data in his book titled "Give and Take," which shows that those who consistently aid others are more successful in the long term.

Giving here does not have to take the form of monetary contributions. You might provide your time, guidance, support, or knowledge, among other things. This idea is often shown on the websites of many companies. Let's imagine you're interested in purchasing a product that will help you shed some pounds. You go to one website, which only provides you with a list of their items along with the advantages of using them.

The second page begins by providing you with details on your current weight. It gives you access to a free calculator that you may use to determine your Body Mass Index. It provides an explanation of what your body mass index (BMI) signifies in relation to your weight and your general health. It provides information on the many elements, such as age, lifestyle, nutrition, and so on, that might impact your weight. You are given access to all of this content prior to making even a single financial commitment.

Which online store will you be purchasing from? Which option should you pick? You will bookmark the website so that you may return to it when you are prepared to make a purchase, even if you do not buy anything right away. You should also subscribe to ensure that you are kept up to date with any new information that becomes available.

When you give to others, you provide them with a sense of worth and appreciation. They will be more than willing to reciprocate when you ask anything of them in the future, whether it be to make a purchase or to participate in a certain cause. Giving first and then asking for what you want is a powerful strategy.

When formulating the message you want to send, keep your audience in mind. It is essential that the style in which one speaks to high school pupils and older people be distinct from one another. You could also need to adjust how people of various genders portray themselves.

Let us take the example of health items; more specifically, let us use the example of weight reduction products. When marketing these kinds of items to women, you may underline how important it is for them to have a body that looks beautiful in adorable dresses, prevent stretch marks, and have a bikini physique, among other things. These are concerns that are very near and dear to them.

It's possible that men won't react as positively to a message framed in this way. It seems that the term "fat" does not have the same repulsive connotation for guys as it does for women. What about getting new clothing that are one to three sizes bigger if the previous ones don't fit? And don't even start talking about how beautiful the beach is. They won't give a damn about anybody staring at them as they strut about shirtless and proudly display their beer bellies on their vacation. They make their name seem more intimidating by appending the word "big" to the beginning of it. Thank you very much for your assistance, Big Austin.

See? A message that is well accepted by the women but not by the men is passed in and out of both groups. It's possible that if you strike them where it hurts (figuratively and physically), you can persuade guys to listen to what you have to say. Make a connection between your goods and sexual wellness. To be more specific, sexual prowess. The thought that they can behave like monsters (or anything close to it) in bed may convince them to consume oats and celery sticks much more quickly. Or anything else that you could recommend.

Do not overwhelm a creative person, such as an artist, with an excessive amount of analytical data while you are chatting to them. You should save it for the corporate leaders. These people are obsessed with statistics and insist that numbers don't lie. Creative people become energized when they hear how ideas will be put into action.

Depending on the person you are conversing with, you need to give careful consideration to the particulars that you select to illustrate. These are just a few instances of how the message might be personalized to the individual who will be reading it. The guiding principle applies not just to the realm of business but also to other aspects of life. You should now be able to do the same, depending on the circumstances that you find yourself in.

When people do not immediately favorably accept your message, you must be prepared to speak it again and again until they do. Doesn't it seem like nagging to you? Certainly not in every case. Consider candidates for political office who are making their case to voters. They run their campaign for a number of months, during which time they engage in daily conversations with members of the public and basically reiterate the same message. In the event that they are unsuccessful in winning that specific election, they will run again in the next one and continue to elaborate on the reasons why they think they are in the greatest position to serve the people. Abraham Lincoln, the 16th President of the United States, ran unsuccessfully for office eight times before finally winning the election for president.

There is a certain allure to the kind of guy (or woman) who never stops asking questions. One who does not yield to pressure or intimidation. People are persuaded that he has ideas that will have an effect on their life as a result of his tenacity. Even the most obstinate among them eventually gave up and listened.

How can you be persistent without being annoying to others around you? Continue to rephrase the message in your own words. Change the way you say things. Every time, provide a few more specifics. Create a demonstration or a prototype. Gather all the pertinent data. People are more likely to react positively to anything that can be seen as compared to words alone. Allow the individuals listening some time to consider the facts before continuing the conversation. Keep pounding on that door, and sooner or later, it will open for you in one way or another, no matter what.

You need to speak with conviction if you want other people to perceive things from your perspective. The listener forms their initial impression of you based on your verbal and nonverbal communication, which in turn influences how they feel about you. Confidence is essential whether you are communicating with others, whether it is in front of a large audience, a small group, or just one individual.

How do you let others know that you are confident? First, let's look at body language. Carry yourself with pride as you go. Keep your gaze fixed on the target. Raise and firmly shake both hands. People will become more interested in listening to what you have to say as a result of this. Pay close attention to what the listener has to say when it is their chance to speak. Doze off every so often.

A confident person exudes an air of positive energy that is immediately contagious to everyone around them. It inspires people, and it gets them excited about your ideas. They can see that you are enthusiastic about the concept, which will pique their interest and make them more likely to want to give it a go.

Make it clear to your audience that there is a certain amount of time. The majority of the time, this tactic is used in marketing. What do they say to you, exactly? Be quick, since supplies are limited! This offer is only good for the first one hundred customers! If you buy it now, you may receive a discount! In most of these deals, they will try to make you think that the supply is restricted when, in reality, it is not. They are aware that a feeling of urgency is effective. They are successful in making you believe that being one of the first purchasers and receiving a certain offer would be an honor for you. And it is effective.

Nevertheless, when it comes to topics pertaining to marketing, make sure you demonstrate that other people have showed interest in your ideas or offered positive evaluations of them. In this day and age of social media, you may depend on the reaction you're receiving online as confirmation that there is interest in what you're offering.

Day four: the evolution of language and the study of linguistic philosophy

There are certain terms in the metamodel that did not just appear out of thin air. Alternately, they might be traced back to the philosophy of expression that was prevalent in the 1950s and 1960s. The people have, however, lost the context of the idea of expression, which has led to the confusion of many of these terms. On day four, we will take a comprehensive tour of the metamodel as well as the Milton paradigm to demonstrate any one particular language sequence. Your capacity to employ these patterns in a way that is both beautiful and successful will significantly improve as a result of this.

We are going to put a lot of emphasis on presuppositions and use set theory to describe the role that presuppositions play in the functioning of the brain. Because of the way that our brains operate, all of these linguistic patterns have made their way into language. Therefore, the metamodel is not merely a communication metamodel; rather, it encompasses a wider range of functionality. In point of fact, this is the only way we will ever be able to retrace our steps and return to the version of the world and of ourselves that is hardwired into the brain. You will learn how to utilize your voice to create an assumption out of anything on the fourth day of the course. And now, let's take a look at the assumptions that were "forgotten" from the very first book written on the NLP, The Structure of Magic.

On Day 4, you will get the opportunity to learn about the Triangulation paradigm, which is an upgraded version of the depth and surface framework. The

Triangulation Model demonstrates that human beings are organisms that thrive in social settings. The Neuro-Linguistic Programming (NLP) is often misunderstood and portrayed as a cerebral mind game while, in reality, the focus of NLP is on how you feel. On the other hand, the majority of people only have a little part to play in the NLP. The triangulation model demonstrates that the surface system is a social structure and that in order for us humans to function correctly, we need the assistance of one another. Many individuals have the misconception that NLP is a lot simpler methodology than it really is, as is shown by the triangulation model. Davidson's work (2011)

The Numerous Advantages Of NLP Training

The study of NLP methods and their use in one's everyday life may result in a wide variety of positive outcomes. NLP is not just a collection of tools and techniques; rather, it is a way of life that can benefit you in many different ways, such as assisting you to develop personally, assisting you to achieve success professionally, assisting athletes in performing more effectively in their sport, and assisting you in improving both your mental and physical health overall. This chapter is devoted to providing you with some fundamental insights into the different advantages that may be found if you decide to transform your way of life via the use of NLP methods. These benefits can be found in a wide variety of areas.

Growth on a Personal Level

You may enhance your quality of life as well as your personal performance with the aid of NLP, which can assist you in managing the issues that arise in both the large and the minor aspects of your life. The following are some of the ways that NLP may assist you:

1. Depending on your wants and requirements, you have the ability to get rid of, alter, or take up new habits.

2. At every given moment in time, you are free to pick the mental, emotional, and physical status that you wish to keep for yourself.

3. You are now capable of communicating and interacting with the individuals you come into contact with in a far better and more successful manner than in the past, leaving little to

no opportunity for misunderstandings and distrust.

4. You will have the ability to overcome the obstacles posed by limiting ideas and situations that stand in the way of your personal development.

5. You will discover the wherewithal to go deep into your inner self and access endless potential that you were previously unaware of. 6. You will be able to obtain the outcomes you have sought.

7. You will discover the ability and the fortitude to lead the life that you want and want, rather than a life that is dictated to you by other people, and you will be able to do this.

You will become the kind of person that you have always dreamed of becoming as a result of the advantages listed above. You will have a greater ability to exercise control over the events that are occurring in and with your life.

Strategy For Acquiring Knowledge

It is generally accepted that successful learning is, to a significant measure, the result of the intellectual strategies that a person employs when working toward the acquisition of another psychological or behavioral capacity. Learning methods are one of the seven key classes of techniques that are acknowledged by NLP (James, 1996). The other six fundamental classes of techniques are memory, dynamism, innovativeness, inspiration, reality, and conviction.

The term "learning procedures" refers to the organization of psychological steps and activities that humans go through in order to develop new reasoning abilities and social capabilities. According to James (1996), effective learning seems to take place via the Test-Operate-Test-

Exit (T.O.T.E) input cycle, which is dependent on PC showing. This is the case with every single profitable approach. The technique of the NLP model that characterizes learning involves identifying the unique arrangement of illustrative frameworks that a person employs inside this critique circle in order to acquire psychological or social knowledge. This is done in accordance with the NLP model that characterizes learning.

Methodology, in this context, refers to the unique physical modalities (visual, sound-related, and sensation-related) that a person makes use of in the process of working toward acquiring a certain ability or competence. Methodology is of special essentiality in motivating learning. According to Steerage (1990), preliminary research indicates that there are no discernible differences between genders or races in terms of the circulation of visual, sound-related, and sensation learning modalities. According to Craft (2001), the sensory modalities are considered to be the means by which data is handled, and the mind and the body are considered to be frequently impacting one another. In connection with this NLP technique concept is the research that was led by Gardner (1993) to report that every individual possesses, at the very least, seven distinct types of insight. These types of insight include etymological knowledge, consistent numerical insight, visual-spatial insight, substantial sensation insight, melodic knowledge, and relational insight and knowledge. A worker at a nursery observes that individuals are capable of exceeding expectations in one domain while being unable to do so in the other domains, and that there may be several types of insight.

There is no one learning method that is both widely applicable and completely effective. Certain configurations of original frameworks will, in general, be more appropriate for particular learning tasks, although they may be inefficient in other cases. This procedure is less effective when applied to the task of learning a physical action such as basketball or soccer, which require a more prominent regard for outer visual and sensation experience (Dilts and Epstein, 1995). The task of learning polynomial math or natural science is most successfully accomplished with a method that includes an internal visual and sound-related review of recipes and graphs.

In order to be successful in a wide variety of different types of tasks, it is essential to have a broad range of different learning methods at your disposal. According to James (1996),

NLP holds the belief that it is more effective to develop the capacity to learn via the use of a variety of distinct processes as opposed to relying just on one. The goal of NLP is to develop and disseminate tools that will facilitate an individual's learning of a broad variety of skills and techniques, as taught by a wide variety of teachers.

NLP And Several Other Forms Of Coaching

The purpose of the development of neuro-linguistic programming was to facilitate human activity, the pursuit of objectives, and most importantly, the expansion of one's own capacities. The term "coaching" refers to a kind of instruction that is intended to enhance human performance in areas such as effectiveness, motivation, and achievement. Neuro-linguistic programming and coaching are like two sides of the same coin; they complement one another, draw on each other's strengths, and provide synergistic results that are even more productive than the sum of their individual contributions. Coaching, on the other hand, is a more all-encompassing notion that also incorporates neuro-linguistic programming; yet, the overarching goal of both is the achievement of success and growth that will allow us to get closer to realizing our ambitions. They act as a type of impetus that drives us to go in a certain direction. Coaching has a positive impact on many different aspects of life, including better and more effective management of business and human resources, better cooperation, helping to develop organizations, optimizing our activities, helping us learn about the world and ourselves, helping us ask questions in order to obtain answers, leading to long-lasting changes, improved relationships, and increased self-confidence. It includes coaching that is based on NLP, the goal of which is to achieve success as well as growth. In addition, it demonstrates to us that we are able to replicate and build upon the achievements of others.

Both coaching and neuro-linguistic programming, which is also known as NLP, have the potential to improve not just the user but also the surrounding environment, leading to increased productivity and a quicker pace of growth. It also makes it possible to make better use of one's intellect by assigning jobs to it, asking insightful questions to which we already possess the answers, which is all that is required to effectively frame the message. However, in order to have a thorough understanding of the NLP system, it is required to become its practitioner in order to get results that are not only instant but also long-lasting. Finding your true potential requires a great deal of concentration as well as an open mind. This is not an easy route to take, but it does present us with changes in our brain in terms of how we behave and how we see the world, in addition to changes on a neurological level. It modifies our language, instructing us on how to utilize the appropriate messages to assist us in finding answers, communicating more effectively with our interlocutors, and influencing how people see us. The combination of coaching and NLP is one that should be considered.

In each of these domains, there are practitioners who have earned certification and who teach particular approaches and how to use them in practice. Coaching is a kind of inspiration that may help you make positive changes, improve your training, seek more motivation, and embrace yourself more fully. The integration of the two facets will unquestionably have a beneficial effect on the formulation and improvement of goal setting, as well as, most importantly, the continuous application of those objectives and the upkeep of a steady level of motivation. Which will allow us to keep becoming better at it over time. Do not stop reading this guide; instead, hunt for more sources of information from which you will be able to draw on fresh strategies that you will incorporate into your day-to-day routines.

www.ingramcontent.com/pod-product-compliance
Lightning Source LLC
Chambersburg PA
CBHW052143110526
44591CB00012B/1836